G. D. TRUC

The Man
The Book

illustrations and text by Scott MacLeay

FIRST EDITION

Florianópolis

Robert Scott MacLeay

2011

Publisher's note: This book is a fictional work. The names, characters and incidents depicted are the products of the author's imagination or are employed fictitiously, and any resemblance to actual persons living or dead, or to actual events is entirely coincidental.

Manufactured in the U.S.A.

ISBN: 978-85-912582-0-8

This book is dedicated to my wife Eliana and my daughter Adriane who make me laugh, help me to cope and love me. I am a very fortunate man indeed.

Preface

This book is meant to make you laugh, the sort of chuckle or groan that comes from bad puns or from suddenly identifying yourself in another person's flaws or awkwardness. As a result, perhaps it will make us think a little about ourselves...but just a little.

G. D. TRUC is, of course, a totally fictitious character, but this does not make him any less real. I began to draw him in 1981 as a form of relaxation therapy in the midst of preparing a major photographic exhibition in Paris. I played around with the idea for several months in my spare time, even made some t-shirts and then, for reasons that are too distant to recall, I abandoned him to a forgotten drawer in my studio. I rediscovered him while working on the construction of the website devoted to my photographic and musical creations last year and decided that he was too much fun to forget. I reworked the character, created new concepts, added colour to some of the original drawings and made some new digital graphics. Before I knew it, there was enough material for this book.

My sincere and loving thanks to Norma MacLeay, my devoted mother and text editor who at 90 years of age is still as sharp as ever. Many thanks as well to my dear friend Ted Scott for his valuable support and encouragement in setting this project in motion. Lastly, I would like to express my heartfelt appreciation to the people of Paris who made my three-decade stay a memorable one. There is something truly enchanting about their city.

The book finds its inspiration in 30 years of living and working in Paris, observing and dealing with the French, their administration and their culture...genuinely loving some moments, thoroughly detesting others and all-in-all, finding the entire experience an enriching one on a multitude of levels. It is always easy to poke fun at strong-willed people of distinctive character. I hope the people of Paris will forgive my inability to resist doing just that in the present volume.

I look forward to the pleasure of returning as a tourist one day. In the meantime, I am alive and well and living in beautiful Florianópolis, Brazil.

Life is a samba.

Scott MacLeay, August 2011

Contents

Preface by Scott MacLeay..VI

Introduction by G. D. Truc..8

Sportsman..9

Seducer...19

Parisian Vignettes..27

Artist..37

Quotes..45

About the Author..62

Ordering fine art prints & memorabilia............................63

Special Bonus Portrait of G. D. Truc................................64

Introduction

The author, a certain Scott MacLeay, has allowed me to write this introduction (a privilege usually reserved for the author) because I am, by all accounts, a very remarkable person. I cannot help it. I know it is annoying, I know it makes me immensely unpopular in some circles, but try as I might to keep a low profile and go about my daily business with the discretion I so ardently admire in others, it is simply to no avail. I am a born leader, a modern-day social magus, a source of profound spirituality and one hell of a charmer. By the way, I am French.

Now you might rightly say, "Hold on, just who do you think you are?" Well I'm G.D. Truc, I studied administration at a very good French university, I am a man of culture, a citizen of the world and I am, well...I am simply better than most people. It's a fact. After all, I hold informed views and I take stands! I'm never satisfied, I strive for excellence and well...as I said, I'm French and as such, I have an inherent sense of the historic moral imperative necessary to make life better on our planet, an organic grasp of the psycho-socio-economic complexities that fester unattended while our leaders deal with superficialities that offer no hope of curing what really ails us. To be quite frank, it is damn difficult being me!

Well, enough of all that. You'll be relieved to learn that this book speaks of none of this. No comments here on the state of the universe, no silly political rhetoric about the art of French posturing (well, almost none), "la gauche caviar" or our cultural and social superiority - just plain fun, because this book is a series of uncensored, snapshot-like quotes and comments - the real me when I am completely relaxed and have let my hair down. We French don't often let our hair down; we just don't like the vulnerability.

I do hope you enjoy it. Please keep up with my news on my blog or follow my tweets. What more can I tell you? Oh, did I mention that I am French? Just joking (not really)!

Grosses bises mes amis!

G.D. TRUC, August 2011

Blog: *http://gdtruc.blogspot.com/*   *Twitter:* *http://twitter.com/#!/gdtruc*

G. D. TRUC

Sportsman

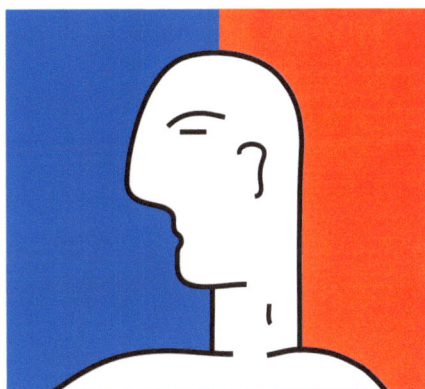

I was very late in taking up pole vaulting.

I first discovered the sport when on vacation in California as a young child. When I inquired as to the name of the sport, I quickly understood that it could never be for me. I was, after all, of pure French origin.

I would learn of my error as a young man many years later during a trip to a football training camp in Warsaw. I promptly took up the sport, achieving remarkably little.

Language is complex.

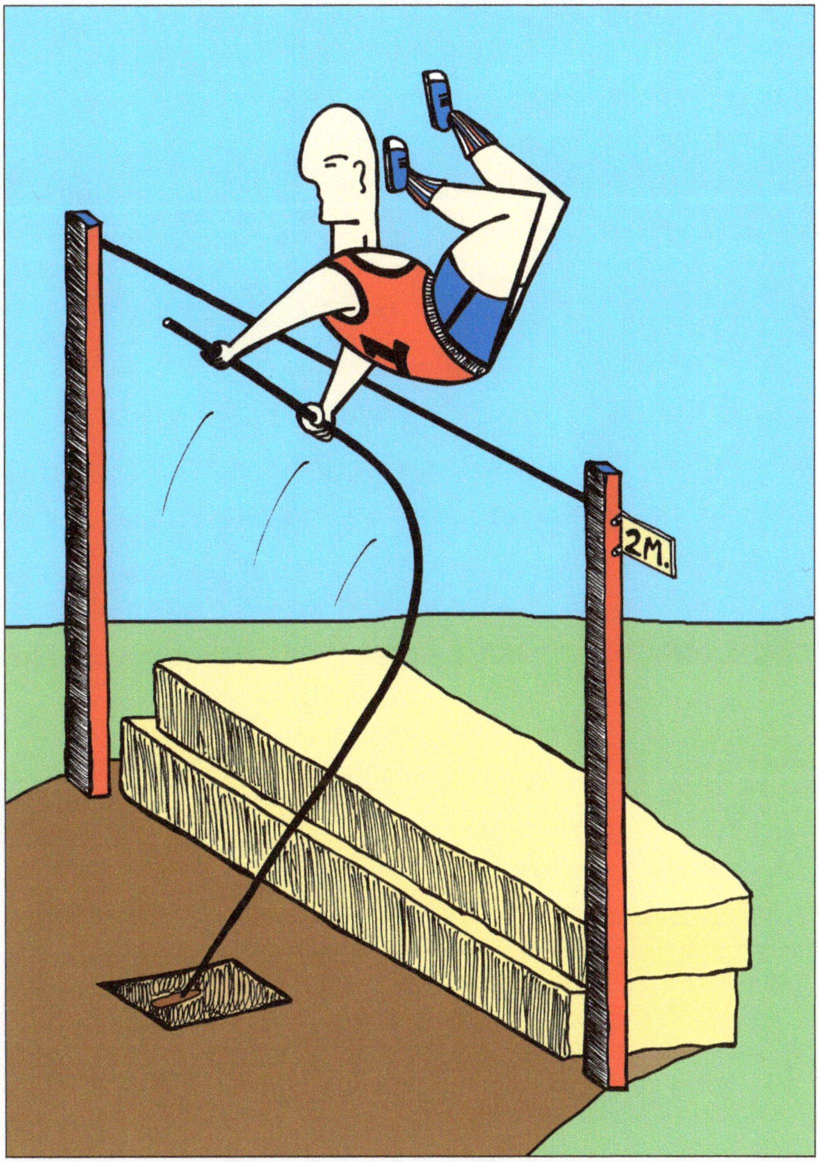
2M.

Posturing is the highly refined, and now almost unconscious, art of taking the high ground when powerless to actually act, thereby appearing noble instead of impotent.
There is perhaps no other behavioural craft that I practise with more confidence-filled gusto than what we French refer to as "le paraître" (literally "to have the appearance of...").

Skiing at winter mid-term break is a perfect example. Imagine the scene! Wave after wave of Parisians, decked out in the latest winter fashions and utterly exhausted after a 500-kilometre traffic jam (generated by a national rail strike), having to get up early every morning to struggle through the same ski lessons we failed to master last year.

Do we care? Of course not, you brainless utilitarian twit! We are not here to ski or to commune with nature! We are here to appear to do these things while seducing our neighbour's spouse in front of our own. It is what keeps us in shape (and we are in better shape than most nationalities). It is quite simply what we do best...appear to do things while doing something else that is likely to be socially (or at least publicly), less acceptable.

Why confront life straight on. I'm at the summit of my art. Oh Mon Dieu! Someone is looking my way! Strike a pose, G.D.!

Life is simply marvellous!

Like all French children, I loved to play football, the game referred to as "soccer" by N. Americans who stole the name of our national sport and applied it to one that is derived from rugby (another sport we French play with more talent and flair than the English). This is difficult to grasp for the Cartesian that I am. The term football applies to a sport in which one can only use one's foot to move the ball, hence the name.

In any case, I was particularly adept at the fine art of goalkeeping. It takes a particularly well-developed sense of timing and anticipation to get to the top and I think that was what made it ideal for me. I was a natural.

I was banned from the sport as a result of match-fixing allegations after a 13 to 2 loss in a third division championship game during which three of our key players were knifed by foreign hooligans as we left the field at half-time with a 2 to 0 lead. I prefer not to comment further.

Life is rarely fair.

I made the mistake of heading out to a public tennis court during a recent visit to Canada. There is nothing like mingling with the masses while staying in shape. Makes one feel as if one belongs. There I was looking smart in my "Wimbledon whites" and to my stupefaction no one even replied when I blurted out with true French exuberance "Tennis anyone?" There was muffled snickering, rude whispering and well…I guess it was all rather humiliating for them to be in the presence of a player of my class. Couldn't really blame them.

Conclusion: Tennis is simply not exclusive enough in North America. Too much democracy, too much access! I like the idea of keeping some things a little more elitist. The people need lofty symbols to which they can aspire. Providing such symbols, I have decided, is one of numerous important elements comprising my destiny.

But I diverge…back to tennis. After this rather crude experience, I felt I deserved a good "gutsy" match against a tough adversary. So I went out and found a private club with a fancy machine… more balls…I like that!

Life is a racket "mon ami", a love game.

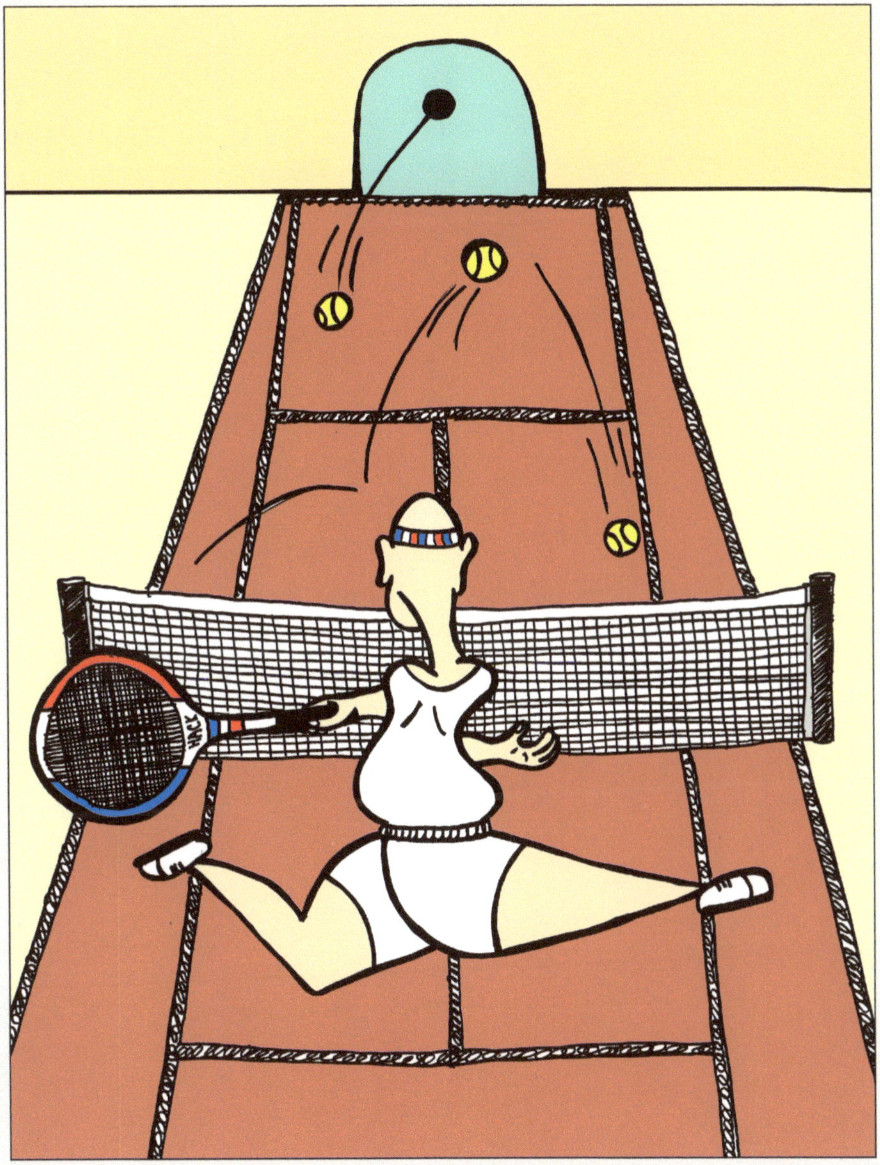
HACK

G. D. TRUC

Seducer

I am irresistible to women when I am on my "moto". I am known in biker circles by my middle name "Don". An international cross-country champion, I have a reputation for being the sexiest man on two wheels. I am considered the best, a King. I know because my groupies secretly refer to me as Don 1.

Biking in France is pure pleasure. Lanes don't exist for us so we can zigzag between cars with no problem at all and at any speed we wish... and it gets better! If uncooperative motorists don't leave us enough space to get by, we can accidently bump off their side mirrors or scratch the side of their cars as we triumphantly fly by.

Now that's what I call "Liberté, Égalité, Fraternité"! "Vive la République!"

But a word to the wise! Never lend your "moto", not even to friends. My friend François lent his to the young son of his best friend David, who, of course, immediately went out and collided with a car. As it turns out the fellow driving the car was completely drunk and so I told François to take it easy on the kid.

After all it was hardly David's son's fault.

Say that again quickly!

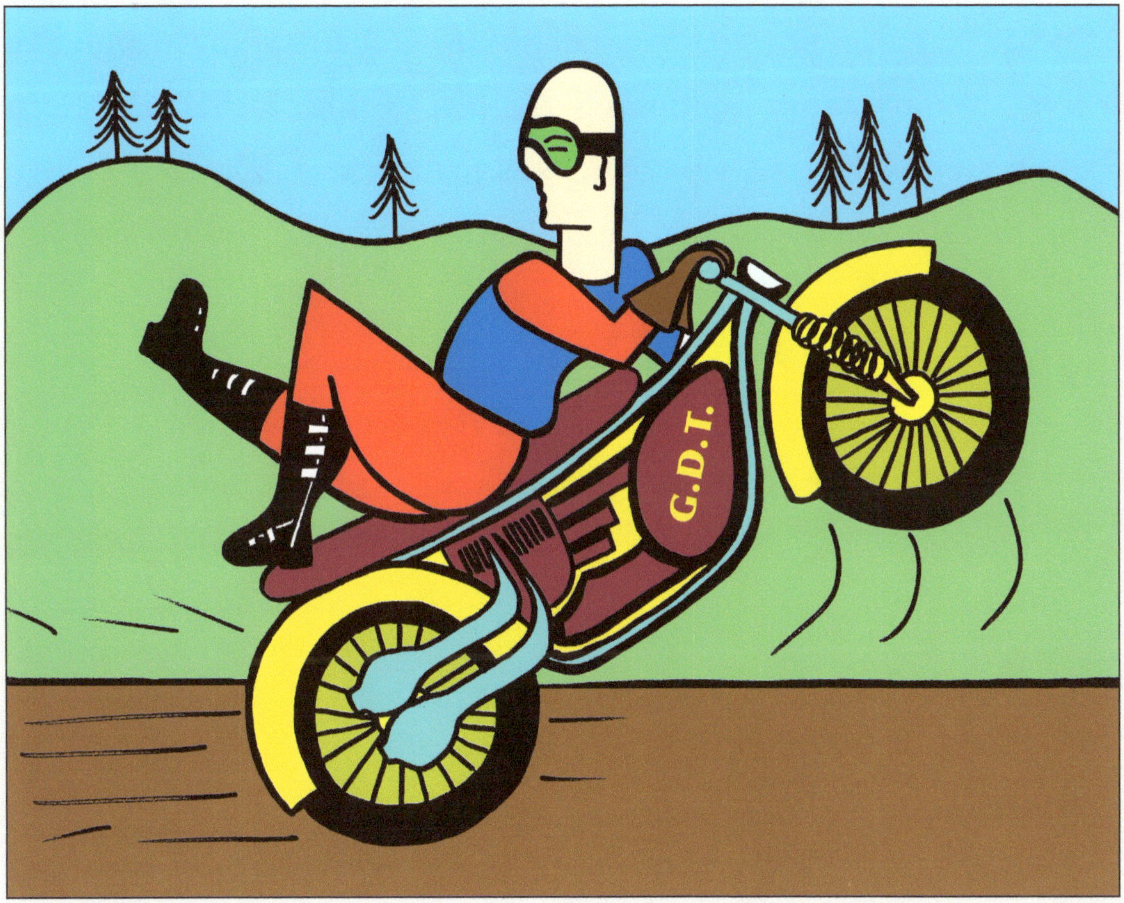
G.D.T.

Love is a complex affair, a challenging chess match!

Rule N°1: Never allow your emotions to betray your objectives - hence the importance of opening gambits in the wonderfully French game of adultery. I have always prided myself on my ability to camouflage even my most amorous sentiments. "Noblesse oblige!"

Rule N°2: Always check on your spouse to ensure that he or she is not going to unknowingly interrupt the proceedings. Of course, we French do not often have to worry about intentional intrusions into our secret lives. Checking on mates isn't part of the game...it is beneath us... it is definitely not French.

Marriage, like diplomacy, is all about... yes, come on...now you are catching on...yes, yes, yes, there you go... appearances, of course! It is a subtle art of discretion and of acts unquestioned and unspoken...

Don't ask, don't tell.

HAPPY SAD ANGRY

JEALOUS EXCITED DEPRESSED

I did this poster for an association that promotes free love and believes in a traditional holistic approach to the art of lovemaking. In fact, it was the idea of the association's President, a Franco-Indian chap by the name of Camil Sutrah, whom I met in India on a steamy overnight train trip to Khajuraho via Agra. We spent the following day admiring statues and discussing the history of Indian erotic art. It was then that he whispered in my ear that he felt my looks were highly suitable for his planned poster campaign. He told me to call his office when I got back to Paris and to make a rendezvous to see Alice, the head of promotion for the association.

As I have stated on many occasions, I believe in getting up for what I believe in and so I gave it my best shot. Several weeks later I discovered elegant effigies of myself plastered on billboards all over the capital.

Cocky old me!

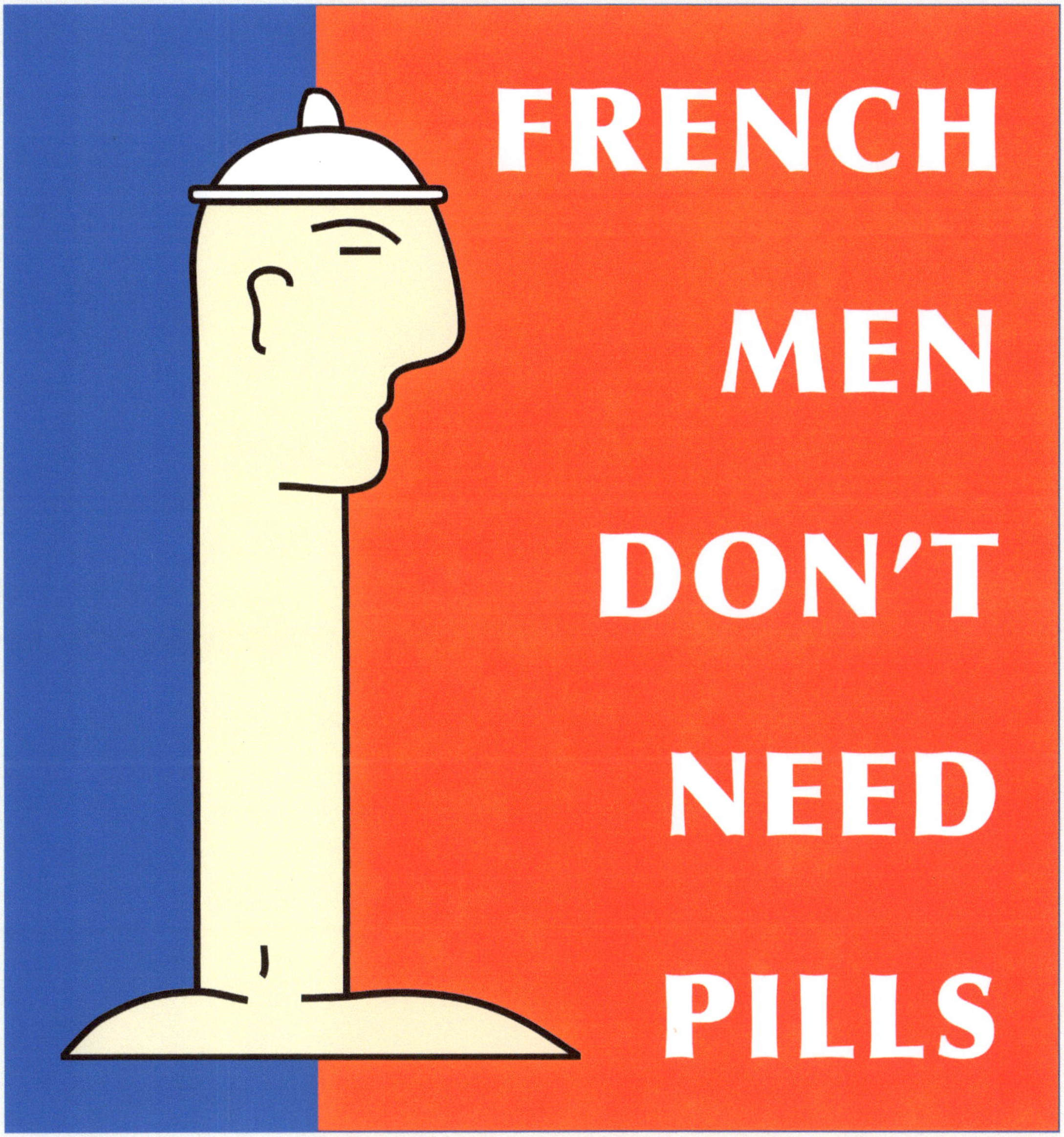
FRENCH
MEN
DON'T
NEED
PILLS

G. D. TRUC

Parisian
Vignettes

Destiny is cruel to those who oppose it!

It is, by nature, persistent!

Destiny

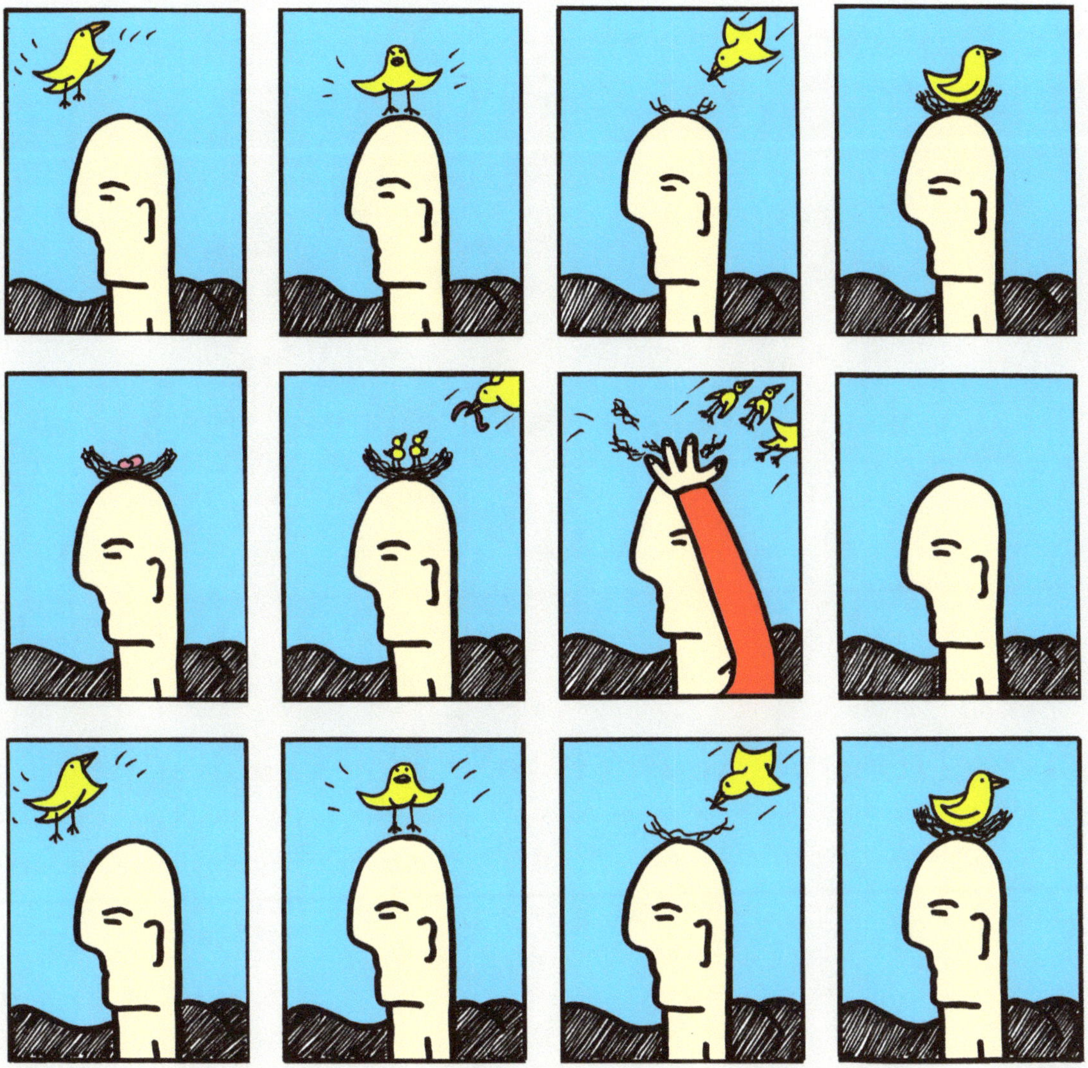

Life is an elevator.

It has ups and downs but really doesn't go anywhere.
That is why enjoying the ride is so important.

Destination fixations are lethal!

Try getting off on floors on which you don't belong!

The Elevator

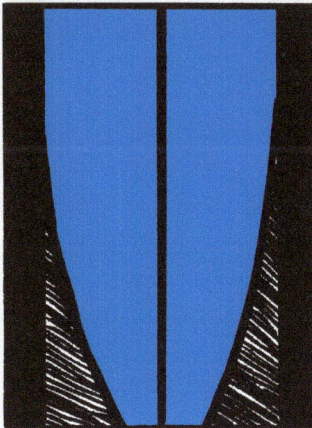
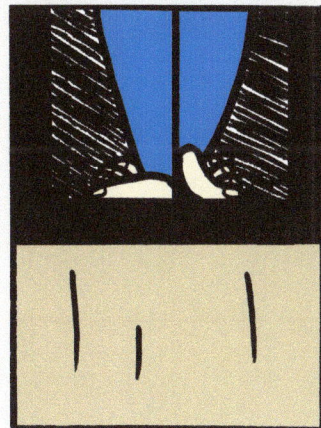

It really is a dog's life.

Paris is the world capital of dog dirt on sidewalks. Why you foreigners make such a fuss about it, I'll never know! Even the municipality feels obliged to act! The most recent official response has been very technological in nature, employing specially adapted motorcycles that tend to spread the stuff very thinly on the sidewalks - sort of like an elegant "tranche" of out-of-date "foie gras" on an old slice of dry "pain de campagne". Such expense for something so natural, so organic, so utterly Parisian!

In the 80's, naive government officials thought that they could inspire owners to have their dogs do their bow-wow movements in the gutter instead of on the sidewalks via a massive ad campaign with the slogan "I do it where I am told to do it." The ads showed a dog doing his thing in the gutter because presumably his master had somehow been able to communicate to him that this is where the job should be done.

Watch your step...oh, "merde alors!"

Bow-wow Movements

SSERIE
SSERIE
SSERIE
SSERIE
SSERIE
PATI

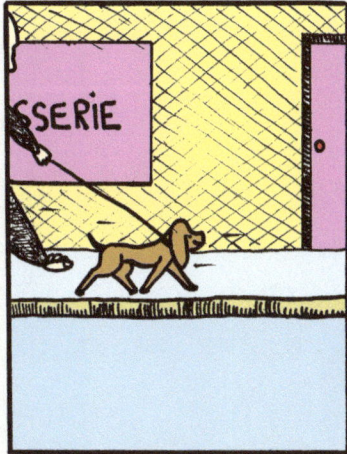

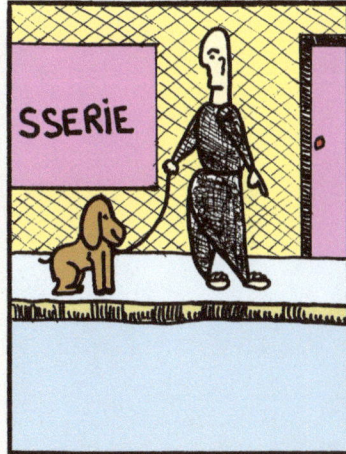

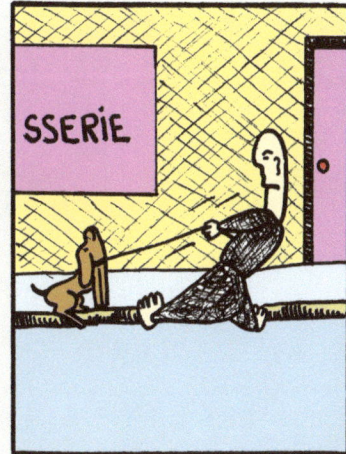

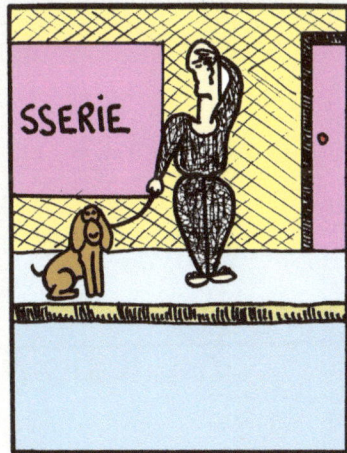

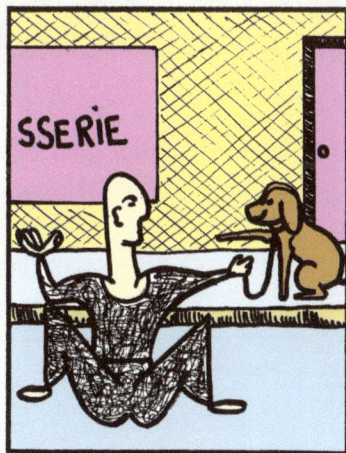

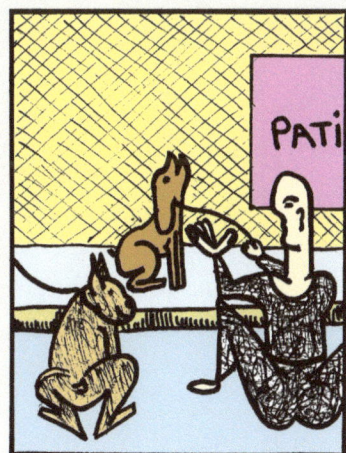

Tennis is a metaphor for life...a delightfully ambiguous game and one in which appearances retain an important role.

For example, the concept of serving is the opposite of what one would expect from its name. It is an aggressive attack rather than a gracious offering. Better still, when someone has "love", they have "nothing". Now there's a scorekeeping concept that I could have invented!

And the more the ball goes back and forth without interruption and within certain bounds, the happier we are - something like counting strike-free days in our public sector.

Yes, one could hold that tennis is definitely out of phase with contemporary lifestyle priorities in the occidental world. I like tennis for just this reason. It only appears gentlemanly, love means nothing and service is aggressive... so very French, no?

Tennis anyone?

The Match

G. D. TRUC

Artist

Me, Myself & I

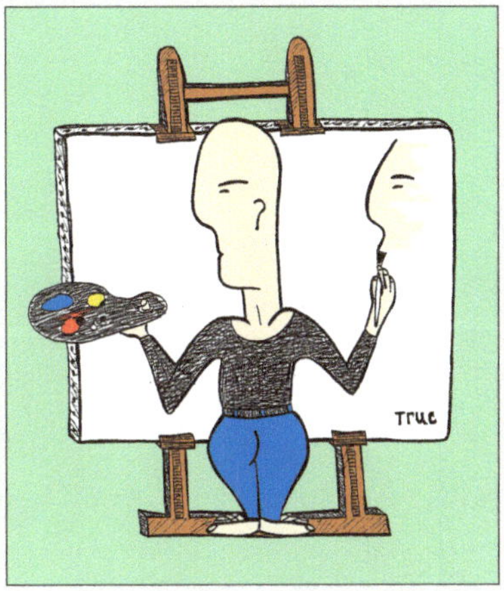
Truc

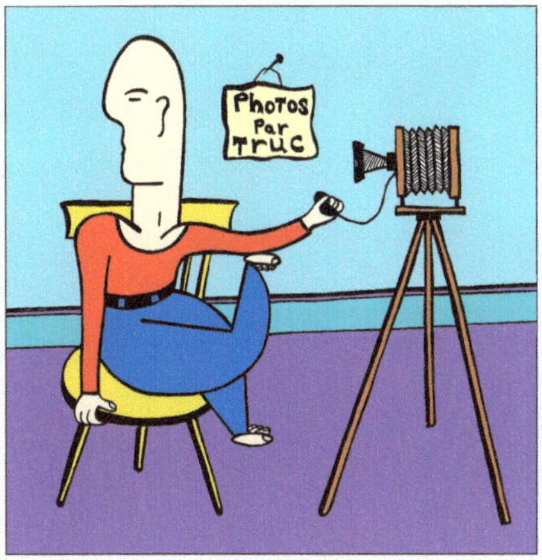
Photos
par
Truc

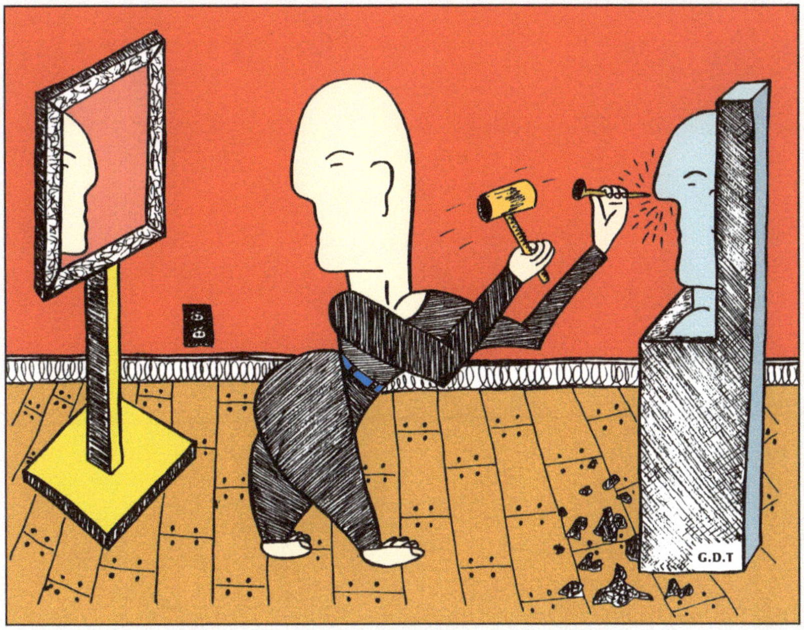
G.D.T

Music is a faithful companion, an ever-shining light.

I expect that this is why literature is so popular in France.

Music is good for the health. Consume without moderation.

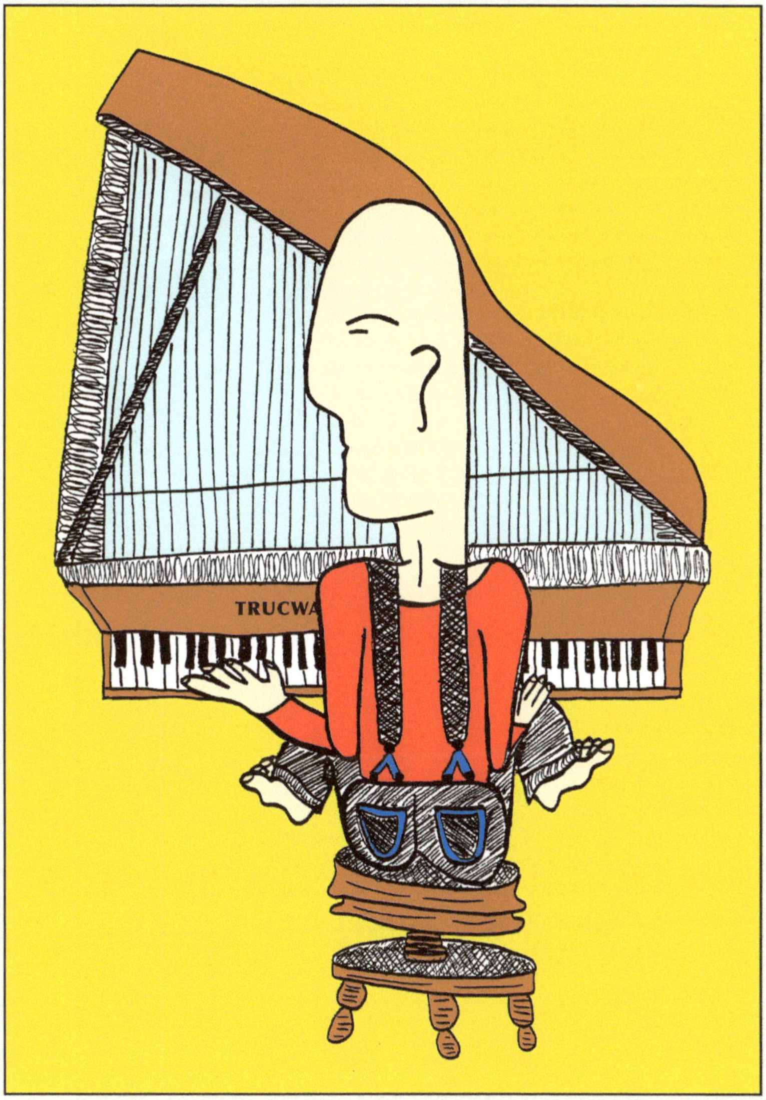
TRUCWA

Dance is by far the most challenging of the arts. Strangely enough, I have never cared for the Cartesian predictability of ballet, its star system and hierarchy, preferring the ambiguity and asymmetry of American contemporary dance with its apparently egalitarian tendencies and intangible themes.

Dance is its own music. It resembles life.

Perhaps this explains why so much of dance is awful.

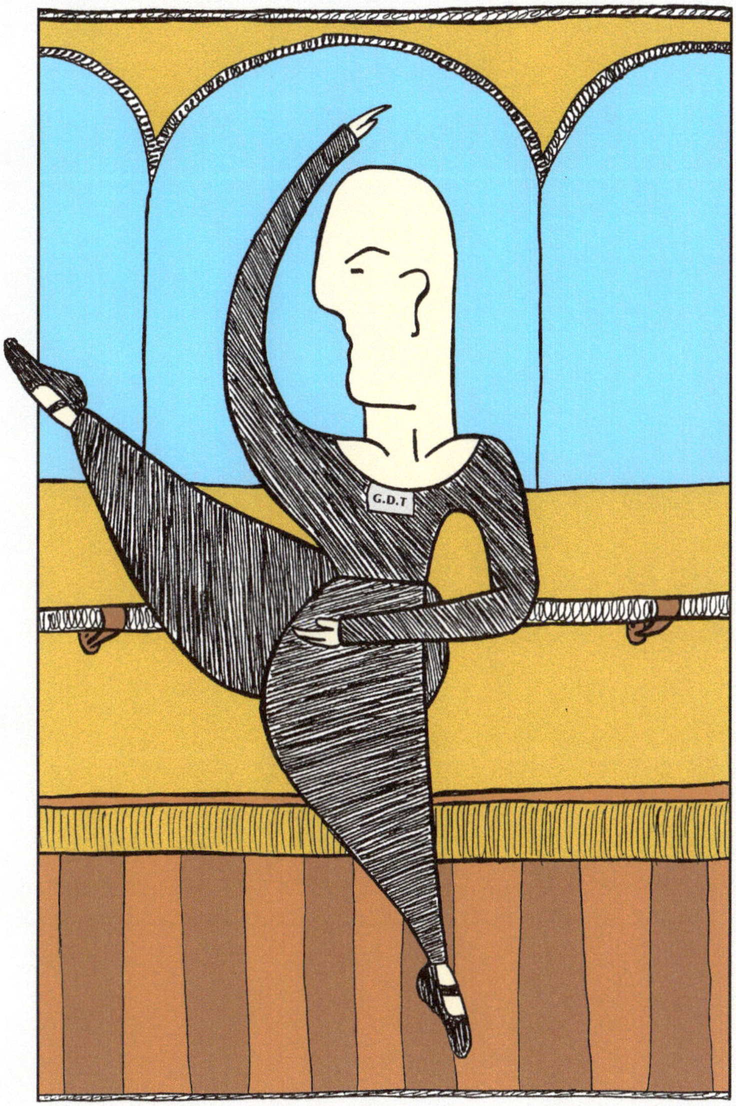
G.D.T

G. D. TRUC

Quotes

Liking oneself is of little value if it is not couched in a profound understanding of how we might have been better and acceptance of why we were unable to achieve it.

There is perhaps no more difficult moral challenge than that of confronting the mirror image of one's self and contemplating the most profound ethical implications of our actions. Best to look the other way lest we discover that our good side is not as bright and shiny as we might have liked.

If the truth be told, it is damn difficult to get along with one's self.

If I was anyone else, I wouldn't be caught dead with myself.

I find this very reassuring.

"Don't try to get on my good side.
I don't have one "

There is something pathetic about a voter convinced he has found the perfect candidate. Poor soul. Does he not know what every French voter knows? That all politicians betray their electorate! Clearly it is impossible to bridge the gap between that which is required in order to be elected and that which is required to survive politically.

In fact, there is only one thing worse than the voter described above and that is several of them in the same voting district. They seem to revel in their camaraderie of ignorance. Being light years away from any form of intelligence or enlightened perception must be bliss. Perhaps that is why the rest of the occidental world is so happy.

I take exception to everything. When I want to know what is good for my country, I seek only expert advice...my own! Being French is the art of being an exception, and of taking exception, to everything. The Art of being exceptional is the Art of being French.

I am the perfect example of this and an exception to it "à la fois".

Any fool knows that politicians don't work. They urn a living.

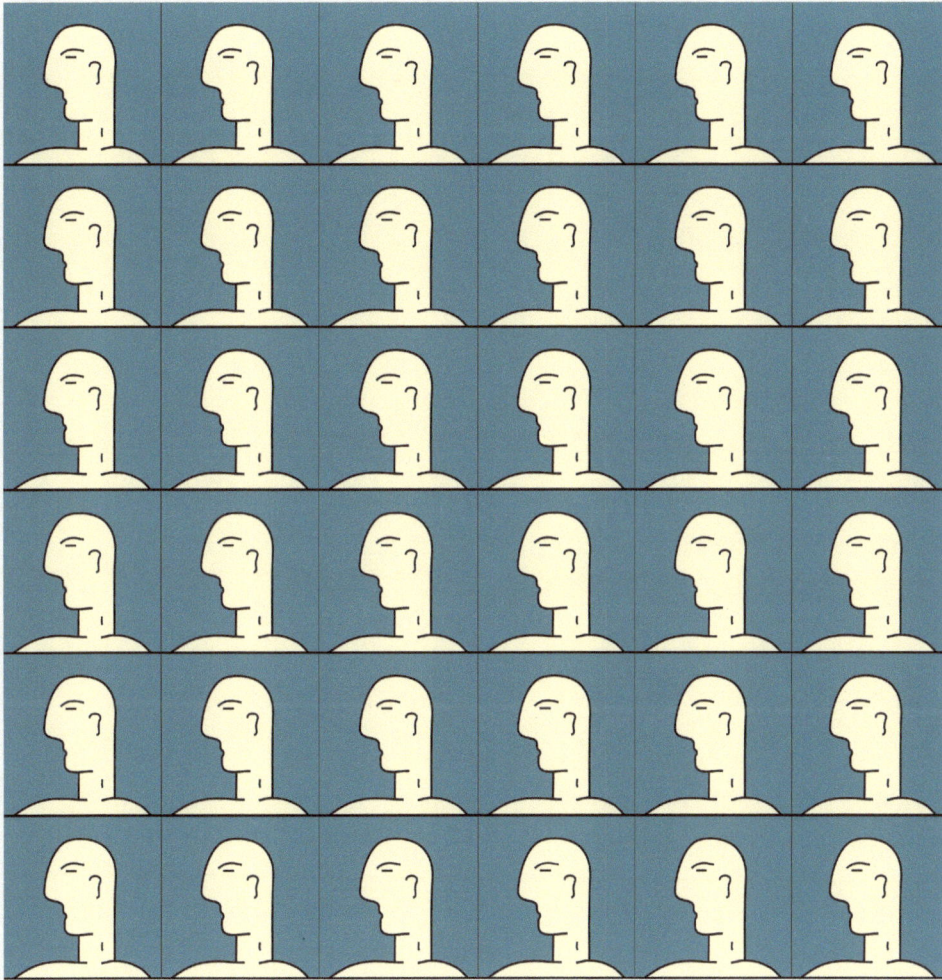

"Dumb, Dumber, Voter"

Profiling bears its name well.

It is for those who don't like facing challenging international socio-cultural issues head-on, preferring to resort to mob mentality couched in eloquent justifications that prey on people's most basic fears and uncertainties as well as on cultural misconceptions and ignorance.

A polarized political landscape with everything either to the left or to the right is profiling paradise...but I forget why.

Hey! Come on! Give me a break! I saw that look! You think I'm just babbling on about things of which I know little or nothing! What was that last comment? No sir, we are not a country of complainers! Well, we don't actually hate Americans, we used to be a bit jealous, but... ok, ok, you are right, we have never really liked the English! And yes, de Gaulle was right about Québec...and most certainly we are more sophisticated, slimmer and better educated than everyone else! What's that? We don't travel much outside of France? If we don't travel internationally as much as our neighbours it is because we have everything we need right here! Even our bread is sexy!

So what are you trying to prove? You don't know me! You are just picking on me because I have a big nose.

We French are naturally high-profile.

"I hate profiling"

Truc's Law N° 1: Sharing with yourself is infinitely more rewarding than keeping things from others. The latter is selfish while the former is simply enriching.

I can hear the cries "But there is no difference. He is splitting hairs". I can't imagine what all this has to do with keeping siblings apart, but no, mindless ones, they are not the same thing...different animals altogether!

The conceptual difference is evidently too subtle for you. It is akin to the difference between the presence of stillness and an absence of movement. These are the subtleties of the highly refined existential lifestyle that I practice daily.

This also explains why Europe as a truly unified entity cannot possibly work. We do not dislike our fellow Europeans. We simply prefer ourselves.

The English have known this all along, haven't they?

This is not a comforting thought.

" Never share what you can keep for yourself "

Truc's Law N° 2: Never face up to a difficulty you can avoid, and this includes moral dilemmas, important ethical judgments, life and death situations, as well as the really important stuff.

This is particularly important advice when there is little or nothing to gain.

The fine art of camouflaging one's lack of resolution with condescending eloquence is, on the other hand, an art worthy of high regard.

It elevates the concept of making the best of a bad situation to a whole other level and keeps the masses quiet.

I call this game "Spin a tale on the donkeys!"

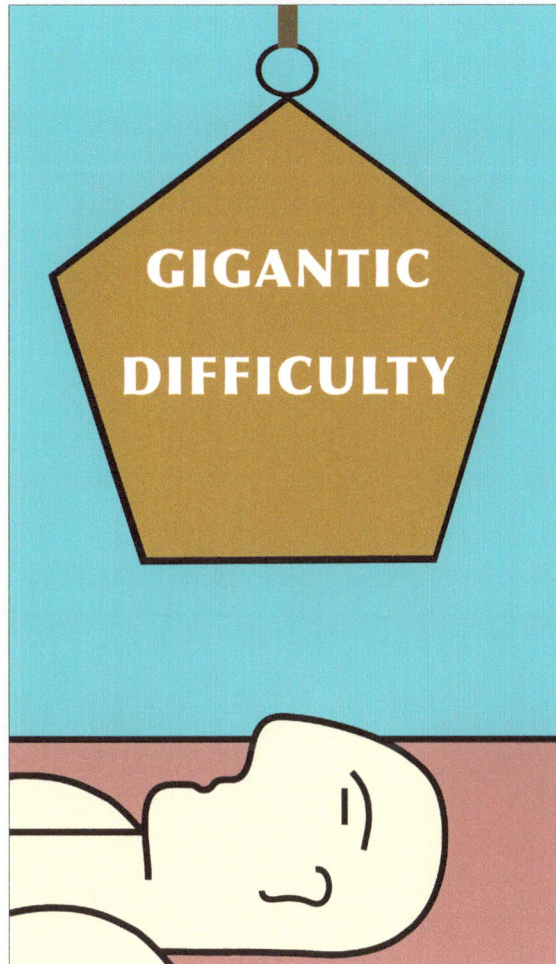

"Facing up to difficulties is often not the optimum strategy"

What can I say about Art.

Probably nothing except that, contrary to popular opinion and to what you might expect from me, I find Art insidiously irritating. It is all-pervasive!

Art is everywhere in Paris...in the cafes, in the metro, in the chic soirées, in the museums & galleries, along the Seine, in the street protests, in the kitchen, in the bedroom, in magazines, on television...Art really is everywhere.

Art is a three-letter word!

" Art is not essential to Well-being"

Ahhh, the sublime feeling one gets from spoiling someone else's day.

I do it to my brother Art every chance I get.

I was wrong...Art is essential to my well-being.

" Never miss a chance to
rain on someone's parade"

Face it!

It is the end!

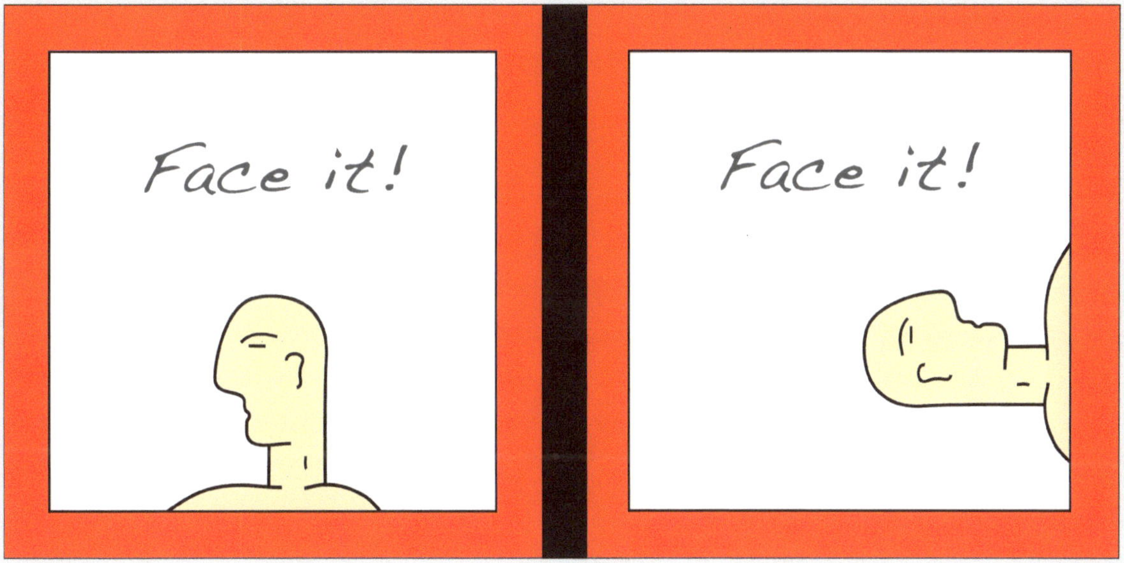
Face it!
Face it!

About the Author

Scott MacLeay is a Canadian artist who lived and worked in Paris for over thirty years. He received a formal education in the social sciences and holds a Master of Science degree in Economic Theory specialising in Development Economics from the London School of Economics and Political Science. He earned a Canada Council Doctoral Scholarship but left these studies at the University of British Columbia to pursue a career in photography in Vancouver, Canada.

Working in fashion and portraiture, he quickly developed an interest in the potential of colour photography as an art form. He moved to Paris in 1979 and had his first major one-man exhibition at the Space Gallery in New York in 1980. For the next eight years he exhibited his work worldwide and was represented by the Marcuse Pfeifer Gallery in New York and the Galérie Créatis in Paris. He founded the Photography Department at the American Center for Artists in Paris in 1980 and became Director of its Center for Media Art and Photography in 1985. He founded the MMAP (Music / Media Art / Photography), a network of professionals dedicated to providing practical hands-on education to young artists in the media arts in Paris from 1987 to 1999.

In 1983 he began composing music for contemporary dance and pursued this work until 1998 composing not only for dance but also for video art and special format cinema as well as for his group Private Circus with whom he wrote and produced two CD's.

Between 1994 and 2009 he also worked as an international project planning and creative consultant on cultural projects in France and in China as well as creating and managing several development projects for European companies in China, India and Brazil. In 2003 he returned to doing commercial photography and advertising design in the spa cosmetics field in Paris.

He currently lives and works in Florianópolis, Brazil with his family. He has returned to working in photography and video and has developed a technological arts development program entitled The Creative Process.

For more information about Scott MacLeay's exhibition photographic work or CD's of his musical creations, please consult the site: www.scottmacleay.com

For information concerning workshops and seminars offered online by Scott MacLeay, please consult the site: www.the-creative-process.org

Ordering Prints

All of the images found in this book are for sale as art prints on acid-free A3 format paper using archival-quality inks. All prints are numbered and signed by the author (editions of 50 prints).

Please contact the author at the following email address for more information on how to order prints: info@scottmacleay.com

TRUC's Online Store

Truc has a fabulous store full of classic G.D. Truc memorabilia. Check it out. You won't be disappointed. It is pure Truc: www.zazzle.com/gdtruc

Bonus Portrait
of
G.D. TRUC

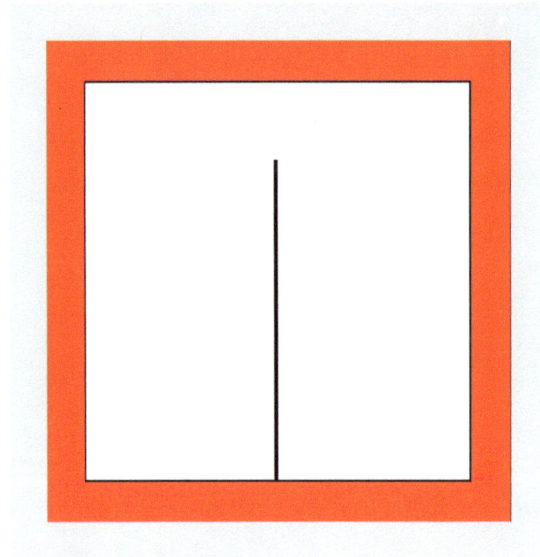

The only existing full face
portrait of G. D. Truc.
Hope you like it!

[signature]

www.ingramcontent.com/pod-product-compliance
Lightning Source LLC
Chambersburg PA
CBHW061048090426

42740CB00002B/75